ANATOMY OF A
DMIN DISSERTATION

ALSO BY THOMSON K. MATHEW

Spirit-led Ministry in the 21st Century (3rd Edition)
From Membership to Discipleship
Ministry between Miracles
Prayer, Medicine, and Healing
A Seminary Dean's Experiment with Servant Leadership
Spiritual Identity and Spirit-Empowered Life
Spiritual Identity and Spirit-Empowered Life Leader's Guide
What Will Your Tombstone Say?
Ministry Research Simplified

[ALL AVAILABLE ON AMAZON]

ANATOMY OF A DMIN DISSERTATION

A Guide to Develop, Implement, and Report a Doctor of Ministry Project

THOMSON K. MATHEW

Anatomy of a DMin Dissertation: A Guide to Develop, Implement, and Report a Doctor of Ministry Project

Copyright © 2025 by Thomson K. Mathew
www.thomsonkmathew.com

All rights reserved. No portion of this book may be reproduced, stored in a retrieval system, or transmitted in any form or by any means—electronic, mechanical, photocopy, recording, scanning, or other—except for brief quotations in critical reviews or articles, without the prior written permission of the author.

Global version published independently in the United States
Available on Amazon

Paperback ISBN: 978-1-7379780-8-4
eBook ISBN: 978-1-7379780-9-1

Cover and interior design: Creative Publishing Book Design
Cover photo: Image licensed by Shutterstock

CONTENTS

Introduction 1

Chapter 1 An Orientation to the World of Research ... 5
The Applied Research Project
Understanding the Scientific Method
Classifying Research Based on Methods
Classifying Research Based on Purpose
Summary

Chapter 2 Problem, Purpose, and Hypothesis 17
Statement of the Problem
Statement of Purpose
What in the World is a Hypothesis?
Types of Hypotheses
Summary

Chapter 3 Anatomy of a DMin Dissertation –
　　　　　　Part 1 29
Concept Paper
Six-Chapter Outline of ARP
Five-Chapter Outline of ARP
Chapter 1 The Problem
Chapter 2 Biblical-Theological-Historical Foundations

Chapter 3 Review of Related Literature
Importance of Literature Review
Chapter 4 Anatomy of a DMin Dissertation –
           Part 2 41
Research Skills
Sampling
Questions
Tools
Instruments
Chapter 4 Methodology
Explaining Method and Design
Next Step
Chapter 5 Presentation of Results
Chapter 6 Responses to Findings
Submission and Defense
How to Write a Dissertation Abstract
Publish Your Research

Appendices 71
Bibliography 81

INTRODUCTION

I have had the opportunity to successfully complete a DMin project and a EdD dissertation. My applied research project in ministry was completed before I had any formal training in research methods. I presented a good report, and it was well received, but my project would have benefited from a better understanding of research methods.

I had a phobia of research in those days, and I could not find anyone to treat it. I have learned since then that this disease is common among clergy of all faith groups, but I am convinced that there is a cure.

To address this concern and to promote more rigorous quantitative research in ministry, reacting to some derogatory comments about DMin dissertations from some friends in academia, I wrote the book *Ministry Research Simplified: A Guide for Doctor of Ministry Candidates Pursuing Quantitative Research*. It was not meant to be a general guide to DMin dissertations but was welcomed as one by many. The feedback I received convinced me that there is a need for a short, easily understandable, and practically useful guide to DMin dissertation to assist students regardless of their math background or the type of research they plan to pursue (quantitative, qualitative, or mixed methods). This book is the result.

This is not original work. I have adapted important research concepts from various texts on research methods in education, nursing, and sociology, to help ministry researchers. The books that have been used are listed in the bibliography. I am indebted to all those sources.

Prior to becoming the dean of the Seminary at Oral Roberts University, I served as the director of the ORU Doctor of Ministry program. This program included a specially designed division for pastors from South Korea who took most of their courses on campus in the United States during summer months and finished their dissertations in their homeland. This effort produced 138 Doctor of Ministry graduates in Korea before the program was closed due to increased logistical challenges. After stepping down from deanship, I have assisted four seminaries in Asia to develop accredited DMin programs as a voluntary effort. Interactions with students in Asia taught me much about the learning needs of DMin candidates from a global perspective. This short guide reflects my new understanding.

Anatomy of a DMin Dissertation

I have used as illustrations some DMin projects completed at Oral Roberts University, and I am grateful to their authors (see bibliography). I hope readers will find the examples helpful.

I have not focused on computations, graphing, statistics, etc. in this guide as I have in *Ministry Research Simplified*. This is not a substitute for regular books on research methods recommended as textbooks in DMin programs. This is a supplemental guide to help students develop, implement, and report outstanding applied research projects to earn their DMin degrees.

I am very grateful to my former colleagues at Oral Roberts University who remain supportive of my continuing academic life, to my students in seminaries in America, Sweden, Korea, and India who taught me much about the power of God's call, and to my wife, Molly, who has been my constant encourager and prayer partner since 1976. I am also thankful to God for my tireless cheerleaders—daughter Amy and her husband Fiju Koshy, daughter Jamie, and grandchildren, Philip and Joseph Koshy.

Thomson K. Mathew
Professor Emeritus and Former Dean
College of Theology and Ministry
Oral Roberts University
Tulsa, Oklahoma, USA

CHAPTER 1

AN ORIENTATION TO THE WORLD OF RESEARCH

Fifty years after its birth, the Doctor of Ministry (DMin) degree is still having an identity crisis globally. Is it a real doctorate? Is it a real degree or just continuing education of ministers? Is it a mini-PhD or a second-class doctorate? I have heard even some theological educators raise these questions in the United States and outside.

It may be enlightening to see the description of the DMin in the manual of accreditation standards of the Association of Theological Schools in the United States and Canada (ATS), considered the gold standard for theological education globally. It states, "The Doctor of Ministry is an advanced, professionally oriented degree that prepares people more deeply for religious leadership in congregations and other settings, including appropriate teaching roles…. The school may offer this degree with specializations or tracks and use those names in official publications…. The Doctor of Ministry degree is an advanced professional doctorate that builds upon an accredited master's degree in a ministry-related area and upon significant ministry experience." (2020, 7). Compare this with the description of the PhD in the same manual: "The Doctor of Philosophy degree is an advanced, academically oriented degree that prepares people for theologically related vocations of teaching and research in theological schools, in colleges and universities, or in other settings appropriate to the degree" (2020, 7).

The Doctor of Ministry is a terminal degree and a fully recognized professional doctorate in the academic field of theology. This is a post-MDiv professional degree. The DMin is not a mini-PhD or a second-class doctorate. It is a professional doctorate like the Doctor of Medicine (MD) degree, especially as MD is offered in Asia. In Asia, a person earns an MBBS degree which prepares him to gain a license to practice medicine. The licensed physician with the MBBS goes to further training to advance his knowledge of the practice of medicine to earn an MD degree, often with a specialization. Both the MBBS and MD are professional degrees, the latter being a professional doctorate. The MDiv is the first ordination-oriented professional degree in the field of ministry. It qualifies graduates to become licensed/ordained to practice the profession of ministry. After a period of practice in the field, the minister can pursue a Doctor of Ministry degree, which is a terminal degree and a professional doctorate. Its primary purpose is not teaching but DMin holders are highly qualified to teach, especially courses related to the practice of ministry, in Bible Colleges and Seminaries.

The Association of Theological Schools in USA and Canada (ATS) considers the Master of Divinity a degree preparing candidates for "ministry leadership." It considers the DMin a degree to prepare candidates for "advanced leadership in ministry." The Doctor of Ministry requires two years of course work equivalent to at least one year of fulltime study and the development, implementation, writing, and an oral defense of an applied research project (ARP). These documents are called DMin dissertations. Some exceptions are allowed in special circumstances to write a traditional thesis instead of a project.

The Doctor of Ministry is offered as a general degree or with specializations in Missions, Leadership, etc. In seminaries offering DMin specializations, about half the required courses will be core courses taken by all students and the remaining courses will relate to the specializations. North America has an organization called The Association for Doctor of Ministry Education (ADME) which advises the ATS on the standards of the DMin degree. I had the opportunity to be a charter member of this organization, which is a great resource for DMin directors, especially newly appointed directors needing professional orientation.

The Applied Research Project

According to the ATS, the purpose of the Applied Research Project is "(1) to apply concepts developed in the curriculum;

(2) to address a practical issue of ministry through research of theological and related disciplines; and (3) to improve the minister's professional skills." DMin projects involve applied research or action research as opposed to other types of research. It is important to have an orientation to various types of research to understand the distinctions of applied research and action research as purpose-based forms of research.

Understanding the Scientific Method

I once heard a Christian physicist say that the ultimate purpose of science is to discover the glory of God. Not all scientists would agree with that statement; most would say that the purpose of science is to explain, predict, and/or control phenomena. While theologians look at scripture, tradition, experience, and reason as sources of knowledge, scientists believe that the application of the scientific method is the most reliable source of knowledge. The scientific method involves the development of a hypothesis (see below for an explanation of hypothesis) based on observations, testing hypothesis, and confirmation or rejection of the hypothesis.

Research is often defined as the systematic application of the scientific method to the study of problems. Ministry research is in many ways more difficult than pure scientific research because it is incredibly more difficult to explain, predict, and control the spiritual aspects of human beings. Even so, the scientific method can be applied toward solving many ministry problems. In this regard, ministry research is very much like applied educational research. Scientific research in ministry, then, like educational research, has the following steps:

1. Selection of the problem
2. Development of appropriate research method
3. Implementation of the methodology/procedure
4. Data collection
5. Data analysis
6. Drawing conclusions
7. Writing and presentation of the study

There are several classifications of research. For instance, research is classified by methods and purpose.

Classifying Research Based on Methods

The following presents the classification based on research methods:

1. Historical Research: This method involves studying and explaining past events. Causes, effects and trends of past events are studied for what they can contribute to explain present events or predict future events. The historical research method uses both primary sources (eyewitnesses or firsthand knowledge) and secondary sources (secondhand information). The authenticity of the data is evaluated by what is called external criticism: "Is this source authentic or reliable?" The usefulness of the information is evaluated by what is called internal criticism: "Is this information relevant to the question at hand?"

   A sample research question that can be addressed using the Historical Research Method would be: "What has been the impact of Clinical Pastoral Education on theological education in the United States?"

2. Descriptive Research: Descriptive research studies the current status of a subject. The method used in this research involves collecting data to test hypotheses or answer research questions. Data is collected through questionnaires, interviews or observations.

   A sample research question that can be addressed using the Descriptive Research Method would be: "What are the self-perceived learning needs of entering DMin students?" In order to answer this question, the researcher has to use certain tools (such as interviews and surveys) to collect data from entering DMin students.

3. Correlational Research: Correlational research attempts to discover the extent of relationship between two variables (a variable is an element or factor of a phenomenon that is liable to change). Correlational studies attempt to establish a relationship, or the lack of it, between two or more variables. It may also use relationships to make predictions. Correlational studies do not necessarily establish cause/effect relationships. Just because two variables are related, one cannot assume that one of them causes the other; there often are other variables involved in the phenomenon. Relationships can, however, be used as a predictor.

   The degree of relationship between two variables is expressed as a coefficient. The correlation coefficient can vary from .00 to 1.00, where .00 indicates no relationship and 1.00 indicates a very strong relationship. Relationships can be positive or negative, direct or inverse. In positive relationships, when one variable increases, the other variable shows a corresponding increase (example: as attendance goes up offering goes up). In negative relationships, increase in one variable produces a corresponding decrease in the other variable (as room temperature goes up attendance goes down).

A sample research question that can be addressed using the Correlational Research Method would be: "Is there a relationship between length of sermons and pastor's approval rating?" One may be able to establish a relationship between the two variables but one cannot necessarily establish that the first variable causes the second. The relationship may be positive or negative. In this case, "length of sermons" is called the independent variable and "approval rating" is called the dependent variable.

4. Causal/Comparative Research: In order to define causal/comparative research, one must first define independent and dependent variables. The variable that is believed to cause an effect or a difference is called the **independent variable**, or the cause. That variable which is affected by the independent variable is called the **dependent variable**, or the effect. The effect depends on the cause; therefore, the dependent variable depends on the independent variable.

In causal/comparative research, the independent variable is not manipulated; the independent variable has already happened. One studies only the effect. Causal/comparative studies cannot establish cause/effect relationships between variables with certainty, as experimental research studies do (see below) because the researcher cannot manipulate the independent variable to figure it out.

A sample research question that can be addressed using the Causal/Comparative Research Method would be: "Do divorced Baptists have stronger pro-choice sentiments than non-divorced married Baptists?" In this case, divorce is the independent variable. It cannot be manipulated; it has already happened. The subject of this research study is the effect of this non-manipulated variable on the dependent variable, pro-choice feelings.

5. Experimental Research: This is the most sophisticated method of research. In this type of study, the researcher manipulates at least one independent variable and then observes its effect on one or more dependent variables. The most important aspect of experimental research is control. Well-controlled experimental research can establish cause/effect relationships. True experimental research requires random selection of the subjects of study. (In a later chapter we will look at different types of sample selection.)

A sample research question that can be addressed using the Experimental Research Method would be:

"Does daily group Bible study reduce the death anxiety level of Korean soldiers who are on active duty in South Korea?" (Jeon, 1996). The group Bible study is the independent variable in this study; the level of death anxiety is the dependent variable. In order to answer the research question, the researcher manipulates the independent variable, which means that he will need at least two similar groups of soldiers. He will ensure that one group (the experimental group) will receive the daily Bible study, while the other group (the control group) will not receive it. This manipulation and control built into this study makes it an experimental study. (The particular experimental design described in this example is called the pretest/posttest/control group design.) If a positive effect is found in the experimental group (that is, if their death anxiety level is measurably reduced), the researcher can claim that the group Bible studies caused the effect (reduction of anxiety), because of the controls and manipulation used in this study.

6. Quasi-Experimental Method: This is a form of experimental research. Ministry researchers can thank God for this method, because it gives some freedom to researchers whose contexts are not conducive to the rigid requirements of pure experimental research. The quasi-experimental method allows the use of non-randomly selected participants, while providing an acceptable level of other controls.

Classifying Research Based on Purpose

Two criteria are used in classifying research by purpose: first, the degree to which the findings have application in the field, and second, the degree to which the results can be generalized. Both depend on the degree of control maintained in the implementation of the research.

There are five types of research based on purpose:

1. Basic Research: Research conducted primarily to develop and/or refine theory.

2. Evaluation Research: Research conducted to facilitate decision making regarding two or more alternative actions.

3. Action Research: Research conducted to solve problems through the application of the scientific method in specific contexts.

4. Research and Development (R&D): Research conducted for the purpose of developing new products or models to be used in a field.

5. Applied Research: Research conducted for the purpose of applying theory and evaluating its usefulness to solve problems. Remember that (practical) theology is theory for ministry researchers.

The Doctor of Ministry requires an applied research project or a project based on action research. I hope seeing the application of the scientific method to solve problems through different types of method-based and purpose-based research will give the new researcher a good understanding of applied research (or action research) as a form of problem-solving inquiry that is vital to the development and implementation of the DMin project and the writing of the DMin dissertation.

Summary

In this chapter we looked at the distinctiveness of Doctor of Ministry as a professional doctorate and the DMin dissertation as a written report of an applied research project. To understand the distinctiveness of applied research, we looked at method-based and purpose-based ways of applying the scientific method to the investigation of ministry problems. There are six classifications based on methods and five based on purpose. Each classification has been defined in this chapter, and some examples have been given. Independent and dependent variables were also defined.

CHAPTER 2

PROBLEM, PURPOSE, AND HYPOTHESIS

There is much misunderstanding regarding the idea of applied research among theological students. Some think they must become scientists to do any research. Others think they must become experts on scientific methods to do responsible ministry research. Still others think they must become technical experts in statistics and must necessarily prove something through their inquiry to call it research. None of this is true. One does not need to be an expert in all research methods or statistical software to do good research. Only a basic understanding of research concepts is required, and a willingness to give up "evangelastic" (imprecise) approach to problem solving. Simply select a researchable topic and follow common sense. There is nothing wrong with seeking consultation if you ever need some kind of technical help. Just recognize that your discomfort is because research is a different world than the one you are accustomed to. Once oriented, it is possible to thrive in this new world.

Just remember that research is not a sermon. It is not a presentation of personal convictions. It is not a good presentation of one's own opinion on a topic. You don't need to be defensive and polemical about your study. Neither is it a compilation of quotations or abridged versions of other people's ideas. Research is a systematic "search" of a specific topic, reviewing and generating adequate information, seeking reliable knowledge.

All research begins with a problem or a question. Ministry research is no different. Doctor of Ministry dissertations begin with a problem in the practice of ministry. Any minister worth his salt will tell you that the practice of ministry has its problems. From inclusive language to fallen evangelists, ministry is full of problems. Ministry researchers often encounter too many problems at once or a problem too complex for investigation. Some ministry researchers remind me of the snake charmers I have seen in India, trying to charm too many snakes at a time. It is a frightening sight. Most snake charmers handle one snake at a time. If a second snake gets out of the basket, they will charm it back into the basket without losing focus on the first one. This is a good model for researchers: tackle one problem at a time.

Statement of the Problem

Not all problems are researchable, so your first job is to examine the major problem area you are concerned about until you find the part of the bigger problem area that really concerns you. You must choose a researchable, clear, interesting, and ethically feasible problem. There is a simple way to check the clarity of a problem: If you can state your problem in one sentence, you do have a clear problem. Whether it is researchable, however, depends on whether your problem involves measurable and/or documentable phenomena (variables).

One DMin researcher was concerned about the problem of evangelism in New York City. He wanted to disciple members of his church for the purpose of improving evangelism in New York City. He began by saying that poor evangelism by his church members in New York City was his problem. During discussion with his peers, however, his problem seemed to change; he began to say that his problem was the lack of discipleship among his church members. After a while the problem changed again. He then realized that he did not have a problem yet. He only had a problem area. It took much more thinking and reflection before he was able to come up with a researchable problem. Finally, he was able to state his problem clearly in one sentence. His final problem for research was the lack of church members trained in evangelism (Daniel, 1995).

Another researcher, a Bible School president, started with a similar problem area and went through a similar evolution in his thinking. His final project dealt with the impact of mentoring on the discipling and evangelistic practices of Bible School students (Samuel, 1993).

Good research problems are not only clear, but they are also limited and specific. There is no limitless research, all research needs specificity and limits. Limitations of the research must be specifically reported in the first chapter of the DMin dissertation.

Good research problems in ministry should also have practical applications. The study must contribute in some way to the actual practice of ministry. Notice the emphasis on the practice of ministry in applied research projects. This is different from typical academic doctoral dissertations where, generally speaking, there is an expectation of contributing new theoretical knowledge.

A good problem must also be a problem of personal interest to the researcher. Research is a demanding activity. Unless the researcher is really interested in the problem, it is easy to lose interest and neglect or abandon the work when it gets difficult. The researcher must also be mindful of his resources before a final decision is made on the selection of the problem. Keep in mind that in addition to skills, one needs adequate amount of time, money, and participants to execute a successful research project.

What are the sources of research problems? While social scientists will tell you that the most challenging problems are derived from theory, the richest source of research problems for ministry researchers is the practice of ministry. Another source of researchable problems in ministry is existing research literature, as concluded studies often recommend further research. A review of dissertation abstracts in databases and current journals in related fields can give you many ideas for research.

Choosing a problem from such sources has the advantage of giving you much needed background information. You will be able to avoid unnecessary mistakes while adding new dimensions to previously investigated issues.

Here are some actual problem statements from Doctor of Ministry applied research projects:

1. The fundamental problem (is) how to bring the immense resources of the Christian community to bear upon the vast human needs of the congregation (Wood, 1989).

2. An adequate method for consistently tending the individual needs of the fellowship had never been firmly established beyond the care of the pastoral staff. The basic problem facing Heartland Church was the lack of felt love and care in the lives of the members of the congregation (Salsbery, 1991).

3. Bible Schools and training programs are available. ... but the progress in the field of evangelism ... has been limited. Unfortunately, many of these programs (which do not involve mentoring) are inadequate and incompetent to meet the missionary challenge of the country (Samuel, 1993).

Here are two ways you may start a problem statement.

- The problem of this proposed research is......
- The research problem is......

Statement of Purpose

Problem statement should lead to purpose statement. This requires some contemplation as the purpose statement identifies the focus of the study and clarifies the study's objectives. A well-written purpose statement can clarify the real reason behind doing the research and provide a clear focus for the study by spelling out the specific objectives of the study.

The problem statements mentioned above (from DMin dissertations) led to the following statements of purpose. I will present each problem statement and the corresponding purpose statement to help you see the connection between the statement of the research problem and the purpose statement.

1. The fundamental problem (is) how to bring the immense resources of the Christian community to bear upon the vast human needs of the congregation (Wood, 1989).

The purpose of this project was to develop an intentional plan to provide Christian care for every person in the sphere of influence of St. Paul's UMC on a continuing basis (Wood, 1989).

2. An adequate method for consistently tending the individual needs of the fellowship had never been firmly established beyond the care of the pastoral staff. The basic problem facing Heartland Church was the lack of felt love and care in the lives of the members of the congregation (Salsbery, 1991).

The purpose ... was to equip believers to do the work of the ministry and thus to assist in meeting the pastoral care needs of the members of the body (Salsbery, 1991).

3. Bible Schools and training programs are available. ... but the progress in the field of evangelism ... has been limited. Unfortunately, many of these programs (which do not involve mentoring) are inadequate and incompetent to meet the missionary challenge of the country (Samuel, 1993).

The principal purpose of this project was to observe if (intentionally adding) mentoring to Christian discipling would create an impact in the lives of the participants for increased involvement in both spiritual and evangelistic activities (Samuel, 1993).

The purpose statement can be segmentized into actionable objectives and based on these objectives specific research questions can be developed. Ultimately, the study will answer the research questions. However, not all research requires specific research questions. Many studies require only a clear purpose statement.

There are five characteristics to good purpose statements and good research questions. Good purpose statements and research questions will answer "yes" to the following questions.

Is the purpose/question significant? (Not all questions are worth investing time and talents.)

Is the purpose/question proportional to the researcher's skills? (Some topics require high level statistical and technological skills beyond typical DMin student's background.)

Is the purpose/question proportional to the researcher's resources? (Some investigations will require a lot of money, travel, staff, etc.)

Is the purpose/question manageable in terms of time required and restrictions involved? (Some studies will be beyond the scope of an academic requirement, requiring years of work and/or involving hard-to-get information.)

It is better to consider another topic of research if the answer to any of these questions is "No."

What in the World is a Hypothesis?

Research questions can be presented in the form of hypotheses. But what in the world is a hypothesis? This is the shortest answer to that question: A hypothesis is a "hunch." Let me explain this and show how DMin research can be done using hypotheses.

A hypothesis is a statement of your "hunch" concerning your problem. It is your tentative statement about the relationship of the variables involved in the problem. In many ways it is an educated guess. We may even dare to say that it is like a statement of faith. For instance, in the study I mentioned earlier about evangelism in New York City, the researcher hypothesized that discipleship training will improve evangelistic behaviors of church members. The Bible School principal I referred to earlier hypothesized that discipleship training involving mentoring will produce better disciples than discipleship training without mentoring. These were hunches, educated guesses.

Beginning researchers often say, "I want to prove my hypothesis." Scientifically, though, hypotheses are not proved or disproved; they are, instead, supported by data (observed or measured or gathered information) or not supported. Experienced researchers do not seek proof; instead, they analyze the data to see if the data supports the hypothesis.

You cannot begin the actual research until the purpose and research questions are finalized, or the hypothesis has been formulated, because the most important aspects of your study, such as the selection of subjects, instruments, and procedures, depend on your purpose, research question or your hypothesis.

What does a good hypothesis look like? Here are some clues: A good hypothesis clearly states, in measurable terms, the expected relationship, or lack thereof, between two variables. A good hypothesis is testable. It is consistent with previous research. It is a tentative explanation or expectation of certain phenomena.

Types of Hypotheses

This section is for general knowledge only for most DMin dissertation writers. Just know that there are different types of hypotheses as listed below.

Research Hypothesis: A hypothesis stated in a declarative form is called a research hypothesis. A research hypothesis declares the expected relationship, or lack of it, between two variables.

Example: Men who attend monthly men's fellowship have higher job satisfaction than men who do not attend monthly men's fellowship. (Notice that attendance is the independent variable (manipulatable) and job satisfaction is the dependent variable (this depends on the level of attendance). This hypothesis declares a relationship between these two variables. The data from the study will either support this hypothesis or will not support it.)

Research hypotheses can be stated in directional or nondirectional formats:

1. Nondirectional Hypothesis: A hypothesis indicating that a relationship or difference exists; it does not say in what direction the difference exists.

Example: There is a significant difference in the evangelistic behaviors of discipleship trainees who have a mentor and those who do not have a mentor. (This hypothesis does not tell you which way the difference is found: it does not tell you whether trainees with mentors exhibit more or less evangelistic behaviors.)

2. Directional Hypothesis: A hypothesis indicating that a relationship or difference exists in a particular direction. It says both that a relationship or difference exists and that it exists in a specific direction.

Example: Discipleship trainees who have a mentor demonstrate increased evangelistic behaviors than discipleship trainees who do not have a mentor. (This hypothesis gives you the direction of the difference: mentored trainees are predicted to have a higher number of evangelistic behaviors.)

Statistical Hypothesis or Null Hypothesis: This is a hypothesis stated in what is called a statistical form. A statistical or null hypothesis states that there will be no relationship (or difference) between two variables and that if a relationship is found to exist it is only by chance.

Example: There is no significant difference in the evangelistic behaviors of discipleship trainees who have a mentor and those who do not have a mentor.

The data collected from a study of this topic may or may not support the null hypothesis (Remember, researchers use 'support' instead of 'prove'). If the data shows a difference, the researcher must *statistically* show that the difference is *significant* (really happening, not just by chance) to claim that there is significant (measurable) difference between the amount of evangelistic behaviors of discipleship trainees who have a mentor and those who do not have a mentor. (Statisticians normally claim significance only if calculations show that the chance of this being wrong is no more than 5%.)

Hypothesis testing is the heart of scientific research. Hypothesis testing requires a sample population, measuring instruments, research design, and procedures for data collection.

Data analysis follows which allows the researcher to draw his/her own conclusions about the problem. Quantitative research in the field of ministry also requires all these steps.

Summary

We have examined the issue of research problem development in this chapter. The process of scanning a problem area and then developing a researchable problem was discussed. Statement of the problem and the purpose statement were explained. Research questions and hypothesis were explained. Different types of hypotheses were defined.

CHAPTER 3

ANATOMY OF A DMIN DISSERTATION – PART 1

Let us begin with the purpose of the DMin dissertation as stated by the accrediting association ATS (seen above): The purpose of the Applied Research Project is: "(1) to apply concepts developed in the curriculum; (2) to address a practical issue of ministry through research of theological and related disciplines; and (3) to improve the minister's professional skills." In other words, by doing the DMin research project (ARP) and writing the report, the student will have a concrete opportunity to apply many of the concepts learned in the DMin program. The student will also have the opportunity to do research in theological and related disciplines. That is, the DMin dissertation should integrate a multi-disciplinary approach to ministry practice. Additionally, the student's professional ministerial skills will (should) improve, which will include problem-solving skills through the application of research skills.

Based on this, here are eleven characteristics of a good DMin dissertation: The ARP should:

be ministry-focused
be realistic
have a specific focus
be situation-specific
be time-specific
have theological and theoretical base
try to demonstrate innovation in ministry
seek improvement in the practice of ministry
keep the researcher's interest
use trustworthy evaluative procedures
contribute to the field of ministry

The development, implementation, and writing of the Applied Research Project goes through four phases:

1. Concept phase: This is the phase of developing and writing a clear concept of the planned project (see below). This phase utilizes class interactions and peer input. This normally happens during the second year of coursework and before the last course is finished.

2. Thesis phase: This is when the first four chapters are finished (in a six-chapter dissertation), normally during the third year, following the class work. These chapters are written in consultation with the project supervisor and DMin director. The project should not be implemented without the supervisor's and/or

DMin director's approval of the method/s used in the study. Some students get ahead and implement the project without consultation and many of them run into procedural and other troubles later.

3. Project activity phase: The *approved* research plan/method is implemented during this time. This includes selecting the subjects, selecting or developing instruments such as questionnaires, surveys, etc., doing the groundwork of research, documenting observations, and collecting the data.

4. Results phase: This phase involves analyzing the collected data, drawing conclusions, making interpretations, and documenting these in Chapters 5 and 6 (or 4 and 5 in 5-Chapter Dissertation).

Concept Paper

Having a clear research concept and writing it with as many specifics as possible is a prerequisite of success. A clear concept helps to select good methods and procedures to complete a successful research project. Following is an outline of a good concept paper.

Title

Choose a title that precisely tells the reader what the research is about. Use your peer group to help you with precision.

Introduction

Present an introduction to your research project.

Problem or Area of Inquiry

Give a description of the setting of the project and the context of the ministry problem with necessary background information. Present the problem statement and give the reader an appreciation for the issues involved. Add the hypothesis and research problems, if appropriate.

Importance of the Project

State why this problem is important to you, and hopefully to the community of ministers and scholars.

Proposed project and Procedures

Describe the proposed implementation of the project here. Include as much information as possible regarding the people involved, instruments to be used, and procedures to be followed, and the timeframe. You may change your plans as you work with your research professor and peer group.

Anticipated Results

Describe the results you expect. State the research outcomes you expect at this stage.

Resources

State the resources required to complete this research. Show how you are planning to meet the challenges of doing this study.

Limitations

What are some of the potential limitations of this study? Describe them.

Meanings/Diffusion

What will this study mean to the researcher and to the wider community of ministers? Do you have a plan to share your findings with the wider community?

Definitions

Are there words or phrases you are using in this study that have special meaning? Please list them. Keep in mind that terms like faith healer, prosperity gospel, etc., mean different things to different readers.

Assumptions

Describe the assumptions of the study here, if any.

Some schools call the Concept Paper a Prospectus and require more information than required for a Concept Paper. While a Prospectus would work well for a typical PhD dissertation, I consider the Concept Paper as outlined above a better match for DMin in-ministry students. (A comparison of the outlines of a Prospectus, Concept Paper, and Chapter 1 is given in Appendix 1.)

Let us look at the DMin dissertation as a whole document. Remember that the DMin dissertation is a written report on the development, implementation, and outcomes (results and interpretations) of an applied research project. A typical DMin project report has six chapters as follows.

Six-Chapter Outline of ARP

Chapter 1: The Problem

Chapter 2: Biblical/Theological Investigation

Chapter 3: Literture Review

Chapter 4: Method

Chapter 5: Results

Chapter 6: Conclusions/Interpretations

The six-chapter model intentionally compels the student to examine the research topic from biblical, theological, and historical perspectives in Chapter 2. In this case, Chapter 3 will focus on more contemporary literature and similar research, shedding light on the topic and demonstrating the need for the particular research. This special emphasis on Bible, theology, and church history is justified as DMin is a theological degree involving a muti-disciplinary approach to problem solving. Many schools, however, recommend a five-chapter dissertation by combining chapters 2 and 3 as Chapter 2. A five-chapter outline is given below.

Five-Chapter Outline of ARP

Chapter 1: The Problem

Chapter 2: Review of Related Literture

Chapter 3: Method

Chapter 4: Results

Chapter 5: Conclusions/Interpretations

Anatomy of a DMin Dissertation

Let us take a closer look at each chapter of the DMin dissertation. Chapter 1 should include the following outline.

Chapter 1: The Problem

Introduction
Statement of the Problem
Purpose and Objectives
Hypothesis or Research Questions
Setting of the Project
Background and Significance
Definitions of Terms
Limitations of the Study
Assumptions

You may conclude each chapter of the dissertation by stating what will be covered in the following chapter. DMin applied research project reports normally do not include the summary of methods, results, conclusions, etc., in the first chapter.

It is easy to notice that a well-written Concept Paper can supply much of the information needed to write Chapter 1. Study the Table below comparing the Concept Paper outline with the outline of Chapter 1. Studying this table should take away the fear of writing the first chapter of the dissertation.

THE CONCEPT PAPER	CHAPTER ONE (THE PROBLEM)
1. Title (of the project)	1. Introduction
2. Introduction	2. Statement of the Problem

3. Problem or Area of Inquiry	3. Purpose and Objectives
4. Importance of Project	4. Hypothesis or Research Questions
5. Proposed Project and Procedures	5. Setting of the Project
6. Anticipated Results	6. Background and Significance
7. Resources	7. Definition of Terms
8. Limitations of the Study	8. Limitations
9. Meanings/Diffusion	9. Assumptions
10. Definitions	
11. Assumptions	

Chapter 2 should follow the outline given below.

Chapter 2: Biblical – Theological – Historical Foundations

Biblical foundations

Present biblical themes from Old and New Testaments that inform or enlighten your topic. If there are selected passages that can be exegeted to bring light on your topic, exegete them.

Theological analysis/Themes

Describe how theologians have considered your topic or related subjects and how you are informed by their considerations. What insights are available to you from these writings?

Church historical perspectives

Has your issue of concern manifested in the past? Are there lessons or insights available from church history?

Faith community perspective

Is there a historical or special concern about your issue in the doctrines or polity of your faith community? Share how it informs your project.

Chapter summary

Provide a summary of the chapter, tying together the various elements of this chapter.

The following outline can be a guide to Chapter 3.

Chapter 3: Review of Related Literature

Similar research

Present *evaluative* summaries of similar research gathered from dissertations and journals.

Theories and theoretical constructs

Related research from disciplines outside Theology can be presented here.

Practitioners and practical applications

You can present related information from writings of respected theologians and practitioners.

Expert Interviews

Interviews with recognized authorities can be included

in this section.

Chapter summary
Summarize the chapter in a synthesizing way.

In a five-chapter model, the outlines of Chapter 2 and Chapter 3 can be combined with less content from Bible, Theology, and Church History.

Importance of Literature Review

A research problem in ministry needs to be well-defined and placed in a theological and conceptual framework. The best way to do this is to review all related literature. Literature review is the process of identifying, locating and studying the various sources of information related to the problem. This helps you to find out what, if any, has already been done about the problem. It also will provide ideas about strategies and procedures that have been used to study the problem area, and possibly the particular problem.

The review may begin with the general problem area and move as close to the problem as possible. Some problems may not have been studied enough to produce many direct references to them. New problem areas will require review of related studies that may not directly relate to the problem. Examining even indirectly related studies can help you better define the problem and develop a proper framework for the study.

A researcher must examine both primary and secondary sources of information. A primary source is the original researcher's description or documentation. A secondary source is written by someone other than the original researcher. You should never be satisfied with secondary sources; whenever possible you must look for the primary source, especially if it is closely related to the problem at hand.

You should resist the temptation to bypass this time-consuming part of the study. Time invested in literature review will save you much time in the long run. It can provide valuable information about the type of measuring instruments used in similar studies. A good literature review can also help you interpret the results of your study thoroughly in the final chapter.

CHAPTER 4

ANATOMY OF A DMIN DISSERTATION – PART 2

The Methodology chapter (Chapter 4 in 6-Chapter Dissertation) requires all the details about the process and procedures, instruments, etc., involved in the DMin project. Before the outline for Chapter 4 is presented, let me share with you two important skills researchers need and some additional concepts.

Research Skills

Recall the seven steps of good research of any kind.

1. Select the Problem
2. Develop Appropriate Research Methods/Procedures
3. Implement Methodology/Procedure
4. Collect Data
5. Analyze Data
6. Draw Conclusions
7. Write and Present Study

Remember that based on the type of data involved, there are two major categories of research methods: (1) quantitative and (2) qualitative. Quantitative methods use empirical investigation of observable phenomena using mathematics, statistics, and computation. Quantitative data is in numerical form such as average, percentage, etc.

Qualitative methods gather non-numerical data for the purpose of analysis and interpretation to answer questions about certain phenomena. Adding quantitative data can strengthen qualitative data and vice versa. DMin research is often a mixed model using both qualitative and quantitative methods and appropriate tools.

As you make decisions on your data gathering methods, keep these three terms in mind and ask the corresponding questions:

1. Validity: Is the collected data valid? Do I ask the right questions?
2. Reliability: Is it reliable? Is my study dependable? Can my study be duplicated?
3. Generalizability: Can my study's conclusions be generalized to a bigger population?

In other words,

1. Validity is believability/trustworthiness
2. Reliability is dependability
3. Generalizability (External Validity) is applicability

There are two very important skills all researchers need. They are (1) the ability to gather a good sample (group) and (2) the ability to develop good questions to address the research issue.

Sampling

Sampling is the process of selecting a representative pool of individuals from a larger population for the purpose of studying that population. The sample is used to gain information about the population. The most important characteristic of a sample is its ability to represent the population.

A population is a group with its own characteristic(s) that the researcher wishes to study. The population at large which is under study is called the target population. The researcher hopes to generalize the results of his study to the target population. However, real-life situations often prevent the researcher from having full access to the target population. He is then forced to choose a sample from the available population. This group is called the accessible population or the available population.

For instance, suppose you want to study the tithing habits of United Methodists in the United States. The entire group of American United Methodists is your target population. You hope to generalize the results of your study to all the Methodists living in the United States. However, suppose that half of the United Methodist Conferences in the United States refused to cooperate with your study and refused to give you access to their membership list, so that you will have to choose your sample from the other cooperating half. Then that half is your accessible population.

Sampling is the most important key to generalization. You can generalize the results of a study to a population only to the degree that your sample represents that population. Poor sampling can be very costly. This writer knows an international ministry that built a whole new division based on a research study of needs. The study was done very carefully except for the sampling. Based on the results of the research using the wrong sample, a huge building was built to meet the needs of a population that was not represented by the sample. The multimillion-dollar mega building was underutilized and had to be closed in an embarrassing way as its maintenance added significantly to the cost of running the ministry, all because the sample did not represent the population for which the addition was built!

Sampling has three important steps: identification of the population, determination of sample size, and selection of the sample. There are different methods of sample selection.

Methods of Sample Selection

1. Random Sampling

Random sampling is the process of selecting a sample from a defined population in such a way that each individual in the population has an equal and independent chance to be selected for the sample group. Random sampling is the best way to obtain a representative sample. However, random sampling is normally not possible in ministry research due to several reasons.

2. Stratified random sampling

Stratified random sampling is the process of selecting a sample from a population in such a way that the identified subgroups of the population are proportionally represented in the sample. That is, the attempt is to make sure that the proportion of subgroups in the sample is the same as it is in the population. Stratified random sampling is similar to the simple random sampling, except that the random selection is made from each subgroup, not from the whole population.

3. Cluster Sampling

In cluster sampling, groups are randomly selected instead of individuals. The steps are the same as simple random sampling, except that groups are selected instead of individuals. A cluster is any group that has similar characteristics. In cluster sampling, numbers are assigned to groups, not individuals. Cluster sampling helps to select samples when individual selection is not feasible. For instance, suppose you want to study the God-concept of Junior High Sunday School students. You may not be able to come up with a random sample of Junior High Sunday School students, but you will be able to select Sunday School classes of Junior High students. You will be able to improve the study by selecting these classes randomly. Cluster sampling is the way to go in this situation.

4. Systematic Sampling

Systematic sampling is a method in which individuals are selected from a list by taking every Nth name. The N in this case is determined by the size of the population and the required sample size. There is a difference between random sampling and systematic sampling. In random sampling, each individual has an equal and independent chance to be selected. In systematic sampling, however, all members do not have an independent chance to be selected. Once the first name is selected, all others to be included are predetermined. That is, the people in between Nth numbers are automatically excluded from the sample.

There are ways to make systematic sampling as good as a random sampling. For instance, if the list is selected in a random fashion, then choosing the Nth names may not violate the chance factor totally. The sample may be treated as a random sample in this case. When the process of selecting the list and the process of selecting the individual are not random, the systematic sampling has serious weaknesses.

The sampling methods we have studied thus far are called probability sampling methods. You need to know about two non-probability sampling methods. These are convenience sampling (also known as accidental sampling) and purposive sampling. Most DMin projects use these methods.

5. *Convenience Sampling*

In convenience sampling, subjects are selected simply because they are available. Their selection for the sample is accidental. For instance, suppose you are studying the Bible study habits of newcomers in your church. You decide to choose the first 15 newcomers beginning the first Sunday of next month. You will choose the first 15 newcomers regardless of who they might be. They are selected very conveniently. The selected individuals will be in your sample quite accidentally (forgetting your theology for just a minute!). Your method of selection can rightly be called a convenience method.

6. Purposive Sampling or Judgment Sampling

The purposive method is sometimes called judgment sampling. The researcher pre-establishes certain criteria for selection and individuals are selected because they fit the criteria. The selection in this method depends on the judgment of the researcher. Suppose you want to study the effect of male Sunday School teachers on pre-adolescent girls from single-parent homes headed by females. You have established three criteria: the subjects must be pre-adolescent females, who come from single-parent homes, headed by females. You select sample girls from your congregation who fit your criteria. The method you use can be called purposive sampling.

While most experts prefer probability sampling methods, both probability and non-probability sampling methods are respectable methods depending on the research problem at hand. Non-probability research enjoys much respect in clinical research in nursing and medicine because of the nature of the problems dealt with in these fields. Ministry problems have much in common with clinical problems as well as with problems in educational and other social science fields. Ministry researchers must be comfortable with using nonprobability sampling methods when they are the most appropriate methods for the investigation of their problems.

Choosing a Representative Sample

The most important characteristic of a good sample is that it is representative of the population being studied. Only to the degree to which the sample represents the population can the researcher generalize the findings of the study. A sample should be as large as possible within practical considerations. It should be large enough to represent the population in a meaningful way. These are the considerations:

1. What is the degree of precision required?
2. What is the sampling method used?
3. Is the group homogeneous? (Homogeneous populations require smaller samples.)
4. How convenient is it to reach the population?
5. What are the costs? Are they affordable?

Sample Size

The following general guidelines (from several experts) can help the researcher in determining the sample size:

1. Descriptive studies require a minimum sample of approximately 10% of the population.
2. Experimental studies require a minimum of 15 subjects per group (Gay).
3. Correlational and causal/comparative studies require a minimum of 30 subjects per group.
4. Make sure that the sample is representative of the population.
5. Make sure that the sampling method and size are consistent with the problem and hypothesis.
6. Make sure that the sample will produce sufficient data for analysis.

7. Remember that even a large sample, if selected inappropriately, does not guarantee a good study because it does not represent the population.

Sample Bias

It is quite possible to have a sample which differs significantly from the population purely by chance. The researcher cannot control this. But there are systematic (not by chance) sample biases the researcher must guard against. You may have heard the classic story of the presidential election of 1936. The Literary Digest predicted that Roosevelt would be defeated by Landon. It was based on a sample of voters selected from automobile registration and telephone directories. Unfortunately, in 1936, not all voters had cars or telephones, so the sample did not represent all voters. The problem with the study was a sampling bias.

Another source of bias is the use of volunteers as participants in the study. Researchers must remember that the volunteers are different from non-volunteers just because they are volunteers! They may not adequately represent the population.

Another sampling bias is the use of existing groups just because they can be roped in to the study. Such a group may not represent the population you are trying to study. If such a group is used, the researcher must state it clearly in the study so that his readers can make their own judgments about the study.

Questions

The second major skill required of researchers is the skill to develop good questions to collect the most useful information.

Tim Sensing claims that there are fourteen types of questions one can ask (2011, 86-88).

14 Types of Questions for Data Gathering

1. Grand Tour Questions: Describe a typical worship service at your church.
2. Guided Tour Questions: Of a situation, task, or place
3. Descriptive Questions: For more information about an action, phenomenon, etc.
4. Task Questions: Draw a map to show….
5. Hypothetical Questions: Begin with what if, suppose, etc.
6. Quotation Questions: Ask to contemplate an opposing view or abstract issue.
7. Ideal Position Questions: Ask to envision an ideal situation
8. Knowledge Questions: Seek specific information.
9. Interpretive Questions: to extend interpretation to a deeper level
10. Behavior Questions: To elicit description of experience
11. Opinion Questions: Moving beyond actions to why seeking goals, intentions, etc.
12. Feeling Questions: Affect vs. opinion
13. Sensory Questions: What is seen, heard, touched, smelled, tasted.
14. Demographic Questions: Age, occupation, education, etc.

Tools

Following are the most used data gathering tools of research in ministry. Plan to develop and use the best tool/s to collect the data for your study. Most studies use more than one tool. Data from multiple tools supporting your thesis increases its validity.

NOTE: Read this section knowing that although the development of valid tools is your personal responsibility and work, there are several sophisticated and affordable online platforms available now to administer them. SurveyMonkey, Google Forms, Typeform, Qualtrics, SurveySparrow, Microsoft Forms, etc., are very popular platforms. Some of these can perform very complex calculations and analyses. Consider the complexity of your instrument/s and the features you need for data analysis before choosing a platform.

Tool 1: Survey Questionnaire

The survey questionnaire is the most used, and abused, tool. The questionnaire is the best method when the purpose of the study is to collect data from a large population that may be distributed within a large area. It gives easily quantifiable information within a certain timeframe.

The advantages of the survey method are many:

The cost is minimum.
It is confidential.
Tabulation is easy.

It can be used within deadlines.

Many people can be asked the same questions.

People are familiar with surveys.

It is non-threatening.

It can be repeated for follow-up purposes.

The survey method has several disadvantages as well:

The response rate cannot be controlled.

The wrong person might be responding.

Literacy is required on the part of the respondent.

Hostile responses cannot be gauged.

Production costs can be significant.

No new items can be added after the beginning of the survey.

A good survey instrument is the product of much legwork. The quality of a survey depends directly on the time and energy invested in the design of the questionnaire. Many surveys are poorly constructed and produce useless information that may be interpreted much but for no constructive purpose.

Survey researchers need to have an understanding of the various rating scales used in questionnaires. A rating scale allows respondents to express their feelings or attitudes on a scale. The most commonly used scale is called the Likert Scale. It refers to a rating scale (usually with five options) ranging as follows: strongly agree, agree, uncertain, disagree, strongly disagree. While this is a very useful scale, it does have one major disadvantage: It allows respondents to choose the midpoint, leaving the researcher to guess their real feelings.

Even-number scales, called forced choice scales, prevent this problem. In these scales, which can have six or more options, respondents are forced to express a non-neutral feeling or opinion. Researchers must carefully write the questions or statements and give clear unbiased directions regarding responses. Careful attention must be given to the appearance of the rating scale. Researchers are encouraged to use different types of rating scales on longer questionnaires to avoid bias due to fatigue. Information on additional rating scales such as rank order and semantic differential can be found in social science research texts.

There are several lists of "Do's" and "Don'ts" about survey studies that are available in various research books. Here are some of the important things found on these lists.

"Do's" of Survey Research

Give clear directions.
Give an easy-to-respond-to scale.
Start with non-threatening questions.
Make everything brief but clear.
Use sensible categories.
Use different types of questions.
Give enough space for response.
Give space for open-ended response at the end.
Tell them what to do after completing the questionnaires.
Give it a professional look.
Consult others who know something about surveys.

Plan for follow-up reminder(s)

Offer some reward to responders whenever possible, such as a copy of the results.

Plan for unanswered questions.

Ask only information you really need.

Do a pilot study.

Get a cover letter from a person who can increase the number of responses from your particular population (response rate is very poor these days).

"Don'ts" of Survey Research

Don't confuse your respondents.

Don't make them mad.

Don't ask foolish questions.

Don't use words with unclear meaning.

Don't use language that is too technical for your target population.

Don't ask multiple questions in one item.

Don't set them up for a desired response.

Don't ask the most important questions at the end.

Pilot Testing

Pilot testing involves having a small sample of the population filling out the questionnaires for you. Use the data from this administration of the questionnaire to discover any problems inherent in your instrument. Even before the actual pilot test, it is advisable to have some of your colleagues fill out the questionnaire and give you some feedback. The pilot test can give you enough data to try out your planned tabulation and even some preliminary analysis. If you want the best study possible, plan to do a test-retest strategy with a selected group. You will be able to find out the reliability of your instrument. Your colleagues can serve as a panel of experts to inspect the validity of the instrument.

Tool 2: Personal Interview

The personal interview is a primary information source. This is the oral form of a survey. It consists of five steps: preparing for the interview, starting the interview, conducting the interview (this can be done by telephone), concluding the interview, and compiling and analyzing the results. There are three types of interviews: Highly structured, Semi-structured, and Unstructured. The structured interview is the best form of interview. It has predetermined questions and predetermined order of questions. The semi-structured interview has a mix of structured and less structured questions. The unstructured interview has open-ended questions. They are often used for exploratory purposes. All interviews can be conducted in a conversational fashion.

Tool 3: Interview Questionnaire

This questionnaire is a "paper and pencil" interview. Based on the purpose of the research, wide angle questions or narrow-focused questions can be utilized to get the information. A well-done questionnaire can yield good information, especially about institutional needs. Unfortunately, questionnaires are often poorly constructed and administered. When attention is given to avoiding the problems of the instrument and implementation, interview questionnaires can be and "will continue to be a most useful and most used information-gathering tool available for tapping the thoughts, opinions, and needs of large populations" (Zemke and Kramlinger, 1989, 158).

Tool 4: Focus Groups

The focus group seeks to acquire a set of responses from a group of people familiar with the subject. It is a qualitative study using a questionnaire similar to an interview questionnaire. A good focus group involves 8 to 12 participants. It should have a questioner and a notetaker or recorder. Debriefing of the group at the end of the session is highly encouraged to increase the accuracy of the information collected. Focus groups can be used for primary studies or to develop hypotheses to be tested using more rigorous quantitative techniques.

Tool 5: Case Study

Case study is a learning tool and method of investigation made popular in the United States by Harvard Business School. Business corporations utilize the case study method to gain new understanding of situations and to solve all sorts of problems. The term "case study" has multiple meanings in the field of research. Some experts in ministry research consider it as a whole method for a research study utilizing other tools, including focus groups. Others consider case study as a tool which is only part of another more comprehensive method or design of research. This is especially true when one is dealing with issues related to pastoral care, counseling, etc. Often verbatims of conversations or written reports of experiences, events, incidents, etc. are analyzed by individuals involved in them for the purpose of gaining insights. William R. Myers' book *Research in Ministry: A Primer for the Doctor of Ministry Program* strongly advocates case study as a wholesome *method* for ministry research. Tim Sensing (2011) prefers to see case study as a *tool* that can address the major issues dealt with in all DMin projects: leadership, intervention, and change.

Tool 6: Critical Incident

The critical incident approach was developed by John C. Flanagan, a World War II psychologist, who was faced with the problem of improving military flight training. Flanagan decided to ask pilot trainees who survived accidents to describe what exactly they had done wrong. "This technique of soliciting 'war stories' is the core of the critical incident process. Critical incidents are facts, specific reports of observed behavior from qualified sources, not generalizations of opinions" (Zemke and Kramlinger, 1989, 129). This is a good method/tool to use, for instance, as part of a study of why certain church plants did not become successful.

There are other research tools, such as Simulation, the Delphi, etc., that are beyond the scope of this DMin guide. Details on these tools can be found in books on social science research.

Instruments

Measuring instruments are standard utensils in science labs. Unfortunately, in ministry research you cannot use the measuring instruments that are used in the chemistry lab. You need instruments that measure the types of things you want to measure. Fortunately, there are standardized tests that a DMin student can use if the subject of research warrants. Standardized tests are reliable and valid instruments to measure certain characteristics, such as feelings, attitude, and knowledge. A research study is only as good as the accuracy and the appropriateness of the instruments used in it. So, before you proceed with your research plan, you must seriously consider the kind of instruments that will be used to measure your variables.

Many instruments are already available for ministry researchers' use. Instruments developed in other disciplines are quite often useful in ministry also. It is possible to find a standardized instrument that will be appropriate for your study. This will save you the time required to develop your own instrument and may give you good data with higher validity.

There are some important sources of instruments that are within your easy reach. For instance, any librarian can show you the Mental Measurement Yearbooks (MMY's). These are reservoirs of tests and test information for researchers in education and psychology. Many of these tests are useful in ministry research. These yearbooks will give you important information about all kinds of tests. You will find critical reviews of a multitude of tests and related bibliographies. If you know how to use a dictionary or an encyclopedia, you will be able to use the MMY's; you must not overlook these great resources.

Another source of test information is the Tests in Print volumes. These give you a comprehensive bibliography of all tests that have been reviewed in the preceding Mental Measurement Yearbooks. These will also serve as a master index to all the tests that have ever appeared in the MMY's. Tests in Print volumes also give information on tests that are not listed in the MMYs.

Another source of information concerning standardized tests is Psychological Abstracts. These can lead you to journal articles dealing with measuring instruments. There are also test publishers who can counsel you on the type of instruments you might be seeking.

Doctoral dissertations are a great source of measuring instruments. Doctor of Ministry research projects are of great value to the ministry researcher in this regard. Dissertation Abstracts International and DMin Thesis Index can help you locate useful instruments.

With this knowledge, let us look at the recommended outline for Chapter 4 of the dissertation.

Chapter 4: Methodology

Rationale (for chosen method/s)
State the method/s you plan to utilize in your study and give a rationale for their use.

Rationale for topic
State why this method is appropriate for the topic of the study.

Rationale for methodology used

State why your selected method/s are best for your study.

Research instruments

Name and describe the tools/instruments you plan to use for your study. What are they? What are their sources? Describe them. If you developed the tools, were subject matter experts consulted, and instrument/s pilot tested?

Design

Describe the design of your study. Did you have one or more groups for your study? Who was involved? Why? Mention the strengths and weaknesses of using this design.

Curriculum development, if involved

Say how curriculum was decided, if one was involved. Who developed it or what is its source?

Procedures

Give step by step description of your planned implementation. No step is negligible. Give specifics so that a reader can duplicate your research.

Sample selection

Who are the people in your study? Do they represent a larger group to which the results of your study can be generalized?

Pretest (instrument)

Are you using a pretest instrument in your study? Who constructed it and how will it be administered?

Report on pilot test, if used

Report on Post-test administration, if involved.

Data analysis
What is your plan to analyze the data collected? Are you using technology platforms? Which ones? Describe how you plan to summarize the data to develop meaningful interpretations.

Schedule of implementation
Provide detailed information on the schedule of implementation. Present all steps involved so that a reader can duplicate your study, if desired.

Evaluation of teaching and curriculum, if involved
What is your plan to evaluate teaching, curriculum, and other activities, if involved.

Chapter summary
Conclude the chapter with a summary.

Remember that during thesis phase, this chapter is written in future tense. Once the project is completed, the chapter turns to past tense in the dissertation.

Explaining Method and Design

The content of Chapter 4 will depend on the selected method/s of your study. This section should deal with: (a) the subjects of the study, (b) instruments used to measure the variables involved, (c) the design or structure of the study, and (d) the procedures that will be followed.

You must clearly define your population. The population is the group from which you will be choosing your subjects. Here you should include the size of the population and its major characteristics, as well as the method you plan to use to select your subjects to represent the population adequately.

You must defend your selection of the instruments (such as questionnaires) you will be using. If instruments are to be developed for this particular study, the rationale and the process of such development should be outlined in this section. You must also show that the instrument will have acceptable levels of reliability and validity. (Subject matter experts can validate your instrument if it is developed by you.) If other materials are to be used in the study, such as study outlines, evaluation forms, etc., they must also be described.

The design of a study depends on the purpose (or the hypothesis being tested) and the variables involved. The design also takes into account the limitations of the real-life situation in which the study will be taking place. In this section you will describe the number of groups involved in the study, and whether the groups will be randomly chosen. You can choose from several research designs. Choosing the research design is like choosing the blueprint of a building; it spells out the structure of the building. As a builder makes alterations on a pre-drawn blueprint, a researcher is free to make variations on existing designs without violating the essential structure of the study.

Let me add a few comments about the procedure section of Chapter 4. This section must contain all the steps involved in conducting the study described in the order in which they will be taking place. Sample selection, pretest administration (if any), posttest administration, and all other steps involved in the study must be discussed in detail in the procedure section. Answer these questions:

> Who will administer the instruments?
> When and where will the tests be administered?
> What are the controls involved in minimizing bias?
> Who gets any treatment (instruction, training, etc. if involved)?
> Who does not get this treatment (in research language, manipulation of the independent variable)?

Next Step

So far, you have seen how to write a Concept Paper and then move on to write the first four (or three in 5-Chapter Version) chapters during the Thesis phase. You are expected to submit these chapters one by one (preferably) or together to your supervisor and DMin director for approval. Do not implement Chapter 4 until you are authorized to do so.

Do not develop your own instruments and tools until you finish your review of related literature. It is this review that prepares you to ask the right questions and to include the right items in your surveys, questionnaires, etc.

After collecting all the information (data) from your study, you analyze the data to address your research question/s to fulfill your purpose (and objectives). While the methodology section outlines the researcher's strategy for collecting data, the data analysis section describes the procedures that will be used to analyze the data. Once again, the researcher returns to the purpose of research or research questions (or hypothesis). The purpose or research question determines the method(s) of data analysis just as it determines the choice of design. The analysis may involve simple calculations or summarizations, or complicated statistical analysis depending on the purpose of the study and the expected rigor. [Consult appropriate texts or experts if complicated designs and statistical analyses are involved.]

Several factors determine the type of statistical analysis used. For instance, the way in which groups of subjects are formed (whether by random assignment or by matching, etc.) and the number of groups involved in the study are important factors. The kind of data collected also will make a difference.

It is time to look at the content of Chapter 5 which presents the results of the study without adding any interpretation. The last chapter will give you plenty of opportunities to present the conclusions of the study and to provide your interpretations.

Chapter 5: Presentation of Results

Make sure you relate this chapter to the purpose, objectives, hypothesis, and research questions of the study. Materials must be presented in a sequential and logical order. Carefully craft and include charts and illustrations with narration. The reader should know what the numbers in the charts and tables mean without guesswork. Choose simple tables. The reader should understand the results of the study by reading this chapter. Make sure you conclude the chapter with a summary of its contents.

Chapter 6 will have the following sections. Note that theological reflection is a major part of this chapter. This section and the segment on contributions made to the practice of ministry affirm that your research, although interdisciplinary in nature, is ultimately a theological effort made by a minister of the gospel.

Chapter 6: Responses to Findings

Interpretations of results

Conclusions (Connect with research questions and results.)

Theological reflection (What does all this mean to you, your ministry, church, and global ministry? Prefer third person pronouns here.)

Contributions (Connect your results with any of the findings discovered in review of related literature in Chapter 3. Emphasize noticeable new knowledge about the practice of ministry gained in this study.]

Recommendations:

    To improve the project

    For further research

    For implementation in ministry

Any additional or unexpected findings

Summary of chapter and the project

Begin this chapter with a brief review of the study's purpose and a description of the results from the previous chapter. Try to attach significance to your findings. Your duty is to make sense of the findings, offer explanations, draw conclusions, and extrapolate lessons. Refer to data as you present your rationale for your conclusions.

Consider recommendations based on your findings. Think of ways to sustain the positive outcomes of your study. State personal significance as well as ecclesial significance in this chapter. Consider the implications of your research on the practice of ministry. Try to reconnect with Chapter 2 in the theological reflection section. Reflect on your study based on scripture, history, and tradition.

Submission and Defense

Typical project reports (dissertations) contain several preliminary pages, including the title page, signature page, table of contents, and lists of tables and figures, etc. Any acknowledgments are included in the preliminary pages, along with a brief abstract of the study. The last section of the dissertation contains various appendices and a bibliography. [A handout of the full outline of a six-chapter DMin dissertation is included as Appendix 2.]

Most schools require an oral defense of the DMin project report. Follow the guidelines of your school to submit your dissertation. Keeping your project supervisor and DMin director in the loop throughout the implementation and writing of the project will lead you to a more positive experience at your defense. Best Wishes for a Productive Learning Journey! Happy Graduation!

How to Write a Dissertation Abstract

Theological schools and publishers of research require a brief abstract of the research study. The abstract must contain the most important aspects of the study. A reader of the abstract should be able to understand the research question, methods used, results of the study, and conclusions. The following is an example of a well-written abstract.

ABSTRACT

Richard Dulany Dupuy, DMin

Effect of Training on Job Satisfaction of Chapel Volunteers in a Juvenile Corrections Facility of the Texas Youth Commission

Lillian J. Breckenridge, Ph.D., Supervisor

This study measured the effect of training on job satisfaction of volunteers in the chaplaincy department of the Crockett State School of the Texas Youth Commission. Surveys submitted by volunteers revealed that they were dissatisfied with the lack of training they received as volunteers. They requested training on the following topics:

1. Concerns of an interdenominational chapel program
2. Social/religious factors affecting youth
3. Suggestions for preaching in the chapel
4. Rules for youth in the chapel
5. Rules for taking students to off-campus church
6. Considerations for campus security

The exact content of the training program was the focus of the research. Each area of interest was addressed in the applied research project report. The research determined a framework for the theological and thematic components of sermons in an interdenominational chapel setting and examined the theories on juvenile delinquency that directly influenced the treatment programs at the Crockett State School. A training manual was developed to assist the chapel volunteer with understanding the needs of delinquent youths.

Twenty-eight volunteers were divided into two groups, experimental and control. Training was provided to the experimental group. The effect of that training on the job satisfaction of those trained volunteers was measured and then compared to the job satisfaction of the control group of volunteers who did not receive the training.

The instrument chosen to measure job satisfaction was the Job Descriptive Index (JDI). This instrument was developed by Patricia Smith of Bowling Green State University. The JDI was administered as a pre-test and post-test to both the experimental and control groups.

Among the members of the experimental group, eight improved their pre-test to post-test scores on the JDI, and six members' scores did not improve. In the control group, two members improved their scores and twelve had no improvement. The nominal difference between the groups' performance on the JDI was statistically significant, at the .02 level. The hypothesis that job satisfaction would be increased by training was supported.

Publishing Your Research

It is a good idea to get a summarized version of your research published in the form of a journal article. The writing of a research report is as important as the planning and implementation of that research. Research reports must be written as objectively as possible; for this reason, researchers avoid the use of personal pronouns. Good reports are written in clear and concise language, using third-person pronouns.

When writing your DMin dissertation, you must follow the guidelines of your school concerning writing style and format. Most schools have prescribed formats for the presentation of dissertations; these must be followed strictly. When you consider the publication of your research in a journal, you should become familiar with the writing requirements of that journal. Journal editors will send you detailed information on their requirements. Often these requirements are found somewhere on each issue of the journal.

Research reports, whether they are dissertations or journal articles, are very similar in structure. The main body of the journal article will contain the following, with only minor variations:

Introduction
Statement of the Problem
Statement of Hypothesis
Definition of Terms

Assumptions and Limitations
Review of Related Literature
Methods (Subjects, Instruments, Design and Procedure)
Results
Conclusions and Recommendations
Bibliography

Dissertations and journal articles must be written soberly, choosing your words carefully. Draw your conclusions from your results and state them in non-grandiose ("non-evangelastic") ways. According to Gay, common errors among beginning researchers are (1) confusing results with conclusions, and (2) over-generalizing. Avoid these pitfalls.

APPENDICES

APPENDIX 1

D. MIN. PROSPECTUS, CONCEPT PAPER, AND CHAPTER ONE OUTLINES

Prospectus Outline*

1. Introduction
   a. Title
   b. Ministry Context
   c. Problem and Purpose
   d. Basic Assumptions
   e. Definitions, Delimitations, Limitations

2. Conceptual Framework
   a. Theological Foundations
   b. Theoretical Foundations

---

* Prospectus outline is adapted from *Qualitative Research: A Multi-Methods Approach to Projects for Doctor of Ministry Theses* by Tim Sensing.

3. Methodology
   a. Intervention
   b. Evaluation
      1. Procedures for data collection
      2. Procedures for data analysis

4. Results
   a. Description of anticipated results
   b. Description of how you intend to report the findings

5. Conclusion
   a. Description of how you intend to interpret the findings
   b. Description of how you will discuss implications and significance

6. Resources
   a. Time: Schedules and calendars
   b. Finances and Materials: Proposed budget (if applicable)
   c. Facilities: Availability, Suitability, etc.
   d. Human Resources: Assistants, staff, experts, participants, etc.

THE CONCEPT PAPER	**CHAPTER ONE (THE PROBLEM)**
1. Title (of the project)	1. Introduction
2. Introduction	2. Statement of the Problem

Anatomy of a DMin Dissertation

3. Problem or Area of Inquiry	3. Purpose and Objectives
4. Importance of Project	4. Hypothesis or Research Questions
5. Proposed Project and Procedures	5. Setting of the Project
6. Anticipated Results	6. Background and Significance
7. Resources	7. Definition of Terms
8. Limitations of the Study	8. Limitations
9. Meanings/Diffusion	9. Assumptions
10. Definitions	
11. Assumptions	

APPENDIX 2

DOCTOR OF MINISTRY APPLIED RESEARCH PROJECT CHAPTER OUTLINES HANDOUT

Chapter 1 The Problem

    Introduction
    Statement of the problem
    Purpose and specific objectives
    Hypothesis or research questions (as applicable)
    Setting of the project
    Background and significance
    Definitions of terms
    Limitations of study

Assumptions

Chapter summary

Chapter 2 Biblical – Theological – Historical Foundations

Biblical foundations–OT/NT

Theological analysis/Themes

Church historical perspectives

Pneumatological application/Faith community perspective

Chapter summary

Chapter 3 Review of Related Literature

Similar research

Theories and theoretical constructs

Practitioners and practical applications

Expert Interviews

Chapter summary

Chapter 4 Methodology

Rationale

For topic (why this method is appropriate for topic?)

For methodology (why this/these methods are best?)

Research instruments (what they are, how made or source, etc.)

Design (mention strengths weaknesses etc.)

Curriculum development, if involved (how curriculum was decided, developed or source)

Procedures (step by step description of implementation)

Sample selection

Pretest (instrument) construction and administration, if any

Report on pilot test, if used

Post-test administration

Data analysis (what? how?)

Schedule of implementation

Evaluation of teaching and curriculum, if involved

Chapter summary

Chapter 5 Presentation of Results

Relate to chapter one hypothesis, questions, objectives, or statements

Present material in a sequential and logical order

Include charts and illustrations with narration

[No interpretation in this chapter]

Chapter summary

Chapter 6 Responses to Findings

Interpretations of results

Conclusions (connect with research question and results)

Theological reflection (what does all this mean to you, your ministry, church, global ministry? Prefer third person presentation.)

Contributions: Connect your results with any of the findings discovered in review of related literature in Chapter 3 [New knowledge about the practice of ministry]

Recommendations:
    To improve the project
    For further research
    For implementation in ministry
Any additional or unexpected findings
Summary of chapter and project

Appendices

Bibliography

[*DMin Course: Applied Research Methodology. Dr. Thomson K. Mathew, Professor*]

BIBLIOGRAPHY

Ammerman, Nancy and Jackson Carroll. (1998). *Studying Congregations: A New Handbook.* Nashville, TN: Abingdon Press. ISBN-13: 978-0-6870-0651-9

Brown, F.G. (1983). *Principles of Educational and Psychological Testing* (3rd edition). New York: Holt, Rinehart and Winston.

Conoley, J.C. and Kramer, J.J. (eds.). (1989). *The Tenth Mental Measurement Yearbook.* Lincoln, Nebraska: The University of Nebraska Press, p. 401-403.

Creswell, John W. (2014). *Research Design: Qualitative, Quantitative, and Mixed Methods Approaches,* 4th ed. Thousand Oaks, CA: Sage Publications.

Davies, Richard E. (1984). *Handbook for Doctor of Ministry Projects: An Approach to Structured Observation of Ministry.* Lanham, Maryland: University Press of America.

Daniel, John. (1995). *Increasing discipling skills of a selected group in an Indian immigrant Pentecostal church.* Unpublished doctoral project. Oral Roberts University.

Dempsey, Patricia Ann and Arthur D. Dempsey. (1981). *The Research Process in Nursing.* Monterey, California: Litton Educational Publishing, Inc.

de Vaus, D.A. (1986). *Surveys in Social Research.* London: George Allen and Unwin.

Dupuy, Richard Dulany. (1992). *Effect of training on job satisfaction of chapel volunteers in a juvenile corrections facility of the Texas Youth Commission.* Unpublished doctoral project. Oral Roberts University.

Fowler, J. (2014). *Survey Research Methods.* 5th ed. Thousand Oaks, CA: Sage.

Gay, L.R. (1987). *Educational Research.* 3rd ed. London: Merrill Publishing Company.

Guilford, J.P. (1954). *Psychometric Methods.* New York: McGraw-Hill Book Company, Inc.

Isaac, Stephen and William B. Michael. (1981). *Handbook in Research and Evaluation.* 2nd ed. San Diego, California: EdITS Publishers.

Jeon, Joseph. (1996). *Death anxiety and religious affiliation: A comparative study of military personnel.* Unpublished doctoral project. Oral Roberts University.

Kerlinger, F.N. (1986). *Foundations of Behavioral Research.* New York: Holt, Rinehart and Winston, Inc.

Mayton, K.H. (1989). *Competencies for teachers of independent study by correspondence in American colleges and universities.* Unpublished doctoral dissertation. Oklahoma State University.

McKillip, Jack. (1987). *Need Analysis.* Beverly Hills: Sage Publications.

Myers, William R. (1993). *Research in Ministry: A Primer for Doctor of Ministry Program.* Chicago, Illinois: Exploration Press.

Rasp, Alford, Jr. "A new tool for administrators: Delphi and decision making," *North Central Association Quarterly*, n.d. 48, pp. 220-225.

Rossett, A. (1987). *Training Needs Assessment.* Englewood Cliffs, New Jersey: Educational Technology Publications, Inc.

Salsbery, William Dale. (1991). *Equipping and mobilizing believers to perform a shared ministry of pastoral care.* Unpublished DMin project. Oral Roberts University.

Samuel, John Pathalil. (1993). *The effect of mentoring upon discipleship training in an Indian Bible College.* Unpublished DMin project. Oral Roberts University.

Savage, Carl and William Presnell. (2008). *Narrative Research in Ministry: A Postmodern Research Approach for Faith Communities.* Louisville: Wayne E. Oates Institute.

Schorr, H.H. (1984). *Senior pastor needs for preparing and continuing education as perceived by seminary professors and senior pastors.* (Doctoral dissertation, Northern Illinois University).

Sensing, Tim. (2011). *Qualitative Research: A Multi-Methods Approach for Doctor of Ministry Theses.* Eugene, OR: Wipf & Stock.

Turabian, Kate L. (2013). *A Manual for Writers of Research Papers, Theses, and Dissertations.* 8th ed., rev. Wayne C. Booth, Gregory G. Colomb, and Joseph M. Williams. Chicago: The University of Chicago Press.

VandeCreek, Larry. (1988). *A Research Primer for Pastoral Care and Counseling.* Decatur, Georgia: The Journal of Pastoral Care Publications, Inc.

Vyhmeister, N.J. (2008). *Your Guide to Writing Quality Research Papers: For Students of Religion and Theology* 2nd Edition. Grand Rapids: Zondervan.

Witte, Robert S. (1985). *Statistics.* 2nd ed. New York: Holt, Rinehart and Winston.

Wood, Bruce Michael. (1989). *Christian caregiving: an intentional plan for implementing a ministry of care in the local church.* Unpublished DMin project. Oral Roberts University.

Yin, R. K. (2014). *Case Study Research: Design and Methods.* 5th ed. Thousand Oaks, CA: Sage Publications. 2014.

Zemke, R. and Kramlinger, T. (1989). *Figuring Things Out.* Reading, Massachusetts: Addison-Wesley Publishing Company.

www.ingramcontent.com/pod-product-compliance
Lightning Source LLC
Chambersburg PA
CBHW071252070526
44583CB00017B/2436